# After the Goldrush

After the Goldrush

Peter Carpenter

ISBN: 978-0-9560559-4-1

Copyright © Peter Carpenter 2009

Cover artwork ('The A26') and author photograph © Roddy Paine 2009. www.roddypaine.co.uk

All rights reserved. No part of this work may be reproduced, stored or transmitted in any form or by any means, graphic, electronic, recorded or mechanical, without the prior written permission of the publisher.

Peter Carpenter has asserted his right under Section 77 of the Copyright, Designs and Patents Act 1988 to be identified as the author of this work.

First published 2009 by:

**Nine Arches Press**
Great Central Studios
92 Lower Hillmorton Rd
Rugby
Warwickshire
CV21 3TF

www.ninearchespress.com

Printed in Britain by:

CPI Antony Rowe
48-50 Birch Close
Eastbourne
East Sussex
BN23 6PE

# After the Goldrush

## Peter Carpenter

Nine
Arches
Press

**Peter Carpenter's** fifth collection, *After the Goldrush*, follows *Catch* (Shoestring) and *The Black-Out Book* (Arc). He is a Visiting Fellow at the University of Warwick and was Creative Writing Fellow at the University of Reading from 2007-08. His most recent poems have appeared in *Poetry Review*, *London Magazine* and *Poetry Ireland Review*; he is a regular reviewer and essayist for *Use of English*. He has co-directed Worple Press since 1997 and is currently a trustee for the Poetry Society.

He has performed and taught at many venues including the Aldeburgh Poetry Festival, Ways With Words, The Troubadour and the Poetry Café. He contributed to Iain Sinclair's *London: City of Disappearances* (Hamish Hamilton) and *La Isla Tuerta: 49 poetas británicos: 1946-2006* (Lumen/Random House).

For Amanda, Zoë and Beatrice

# ACKNOWLEDGEMENTS

Acknowledgements are due to the editors of the following publications in which some of these poems, or early versions of them, first appeared: *English*, *London Magazine*, *The North*, *Other Poetry*, *Poetry Ireland Review*, *Poetry Review*, *Smiths Knoll*, *Staple*, *Tears in the Fence*, *Use of English*, *Under the Radar* and *The Wolf*.

An early version of 'The Goodbye Game' was short-listed for the Keats-Shelley Memorial Poetry Prize in 2008; an early version of 'Prophet' appeared in *Catch* (Shoestring 2006); 'Hair of the Dog' was published in a special limited edition by Lamb and Flag Press (August 2008); 'From the Smokery' was part of the 'Poetry Windows' exhibition in 2009; 'Borders' appeared in *Speaking English* (Five Leaves Press 2007, edited by Andy Croft); many of the poems, or earlier versions of them, appeared in a pamphlet, *You Said It*, shortlisted for the 2006 Poetry Business Prize.

I am especially grateful to the following people for their advice and encouragement: Ian Brinton, David Caddy, Kevin Jackson, Tim Liardet, John Lucas, Allison McVety, David Morley, Peter Robinson, Christopher Reid, Peter and Ann Sansom, Clive Wilmer and Joseph Woods. Thanks to all those involved in the workshops at the University of Reading during my time as Creative Writing Fellow during 2007-08; also, to The Poetry Trust (in particular Naomi Jaffa, Michael Laskey and Dean Parkin) for the chance to work at the 2007 Aldeburgh Poetry Festival. Special thanks go to colleagues and students at Tonbridge School, especially those in the English Department and the Creative Writing Society.

Above all, though, thanks to Amanda Carpenter for her unfailing love and support.

# CONTENTS

\*

| | |
|---|---|
| An Unidentified Man | 11 |
| Mister Memory | 12 |
| From the Smokery | 13 |
| The Swing | 14 |
| Keith Standing | 15 |
| Orion | 16 |
| Tour | 17 |
| The Going | 18 |
| Near Ronda | 19 |
| Locust | 20 |
| Lines for the Trial of Saddam Hussein | 21 |
| Sand Person | 22 |
| Facts of Life | 23 |
| Holocaust Exhibition | 24 |
| Namings | 25 |
| Caspar David Friedrich | 26 |
| Santa | 27 |
| To a Pipistrelle | 28 |

\*

| | |
|---|---|
| Prophet | 31 |
| Regeneration | 33 |
| Borders | 34 |
| Settlers | 35 |
| Personal Empowerment Practice | 36 |
| *from* 'The Paddington Cantos' | 37 |
| In Brief | 39 |
| Opening of the Sixth Seal | 40 |

\*

| | |
|---|---|
| Cambridge | 43 |
| Socialist Realism | 45 |
| Reading Yeats in The Granta | 46 |
| The Cambridge Ghost | 47 |
| False Oat Grass – A Figure of Eight Walk | 49 |
| Easterly | 50 |
| Short Stay | 51 |
| Near Death | 52 |
| The Other Poet's House | 53 |
| Hair of the Dog | 54 |
| The Great Elk | 55 |
| Sweetman | 56 |
| Bin Men | 57 |
| After George Trakl | 58 |
| The Goodbye Game | 59 |
| Your Hands | 60 |
| Nightwatchman | 61 |
| Beautiful Game | 62 |

\*

| | |
|---|---|
| The Gift | 65 |

| | |
|---|---|
| Notes | 67 |

\*

> To paint's to breathe,
> And all the darknesses are dared

– Elizabeth Jennings

# An Unidentified Man

He's not petting a marmoset
or stroking the breast feathers
of a hooded falcon.
His hat-badge is blank
and his livery is unknown.

Behind him no roses
or marigolds, no hidden clues
in a fusion of oak and vine,
no sectarian motifs, nothing
to suggest that he's a cleric,
barber or surgeon to the king
or member of the Hanseatic League.

There's no obvious ennui
or resolution in his features,
no helpful foot-note
to say he was imprisoned
for his beliefs, yet still
we share his space,
find ourselves in his presence.

# Mister Memory

Forgive the chemical glaze to the eyes,
the clammy handshake, the *how's it going, mate*,
and for god's sake don't square up to him.
That's close enough. Ignore the soppy grin,
the turned-back Burberry baseball cap
(complete with Cross of St. George patch) –
too late, we're shuffling down Adelphi Road,
him doing his thirty nine steps routine,
and me collared with the Mau Mau, the great
surge of fifty three, whalemeat, those legendary
pre-match antics of Budgie Burridge.

# From the Smokery

Through the miracle of the smokery
it comes out fresh on the enamel plate
a full forty years on, stinking the place
to high heaven. I turn it from pipistrelle
to a woman's leather gloves to giant insect –
a stag beetle, cleavered, legs in the air, opening up
like a good short story.
                        Its armoury of bones
and deflector shields is surely cast in bronze.
A spine to work under and lift clear
with the line of the knife before the flesh
can be enjoyed: the intricacies of a whole life,
worth taking time over.
                        My long-dead grandfather
puts it there in front of me. Windows run
with condensation. The grill's still on for toast.
I make a start as he's creasing flat his *Mirror*.

# The Swing

Simple construction: one sawn branch set between the Ys of adjacent apple trees, cookers, part of the orchard plot divided across the gardens of four new houses. Thick nylon cords to take the plank, three paving stones specially laid into the turf beneath. I'm in my stride, a good rhythm from legs extended up front then feet tucked in behind, rocking the whole thing, encouraging sudden late fallers. Mother's framed against kitchen windows that drip with condensation. Today it's her steak and kidney thing with the suet topping.

I stare out to the crab apples down by the crazy paving and swear blind it's Uncle Jim, vast pleated trousers held up with crimson braces, buffed cherry brogues, collarless shirt, huge rear facing my way. His left arm waves me forward. He's stuck, that's it, like those parachutists at Arnhem, and all he needs is a really good shove on his grand derrière, obvious really.

'Give us a hand, smartish, young Pete, jump to.' I glimpse curls above the short back and sides and those special glasses that turn dark in sunlight. But what about the 'massive attack' that did for him one night in front of the set back there in Worcester Park? It's too late now – he's into an Arthur Askey routine: twiddling the shades between thumb and forefinger, dribbling slightly: 'I'm a-thanking you, I'm a-thanking you, all you lovely people, I'm a-thanking you.'

# Keith Standing

Field mushroom ears. Monday's callus of snot
or mashed potato still there on frayed Airtex collar come Friday.
John Lennon specs bleared by fingerprints, ice-rink scoured;
basin crewcut, involuntary half-grin, right arm braced permanently
in the air. Class fall guy, back-up anarchist when General Science
with Doc Death had passed its sell-by date.

'Sir, sir, I've swallowed some copper sulphate, sir.'

A frothy lisp of ocean-blue cola. Epsom District. Sirens, the works.

You grew on us. A trouper. For P.E. repeated offence:
coal-dust socks, no House vest. Punishment: in sheeting rain
to pick flints off terraced pitches down at Priest Hill. Undaunted,
you deliver them in a sack to Norris's desk like Millet's Sower
in steamed-over cartoon specs. Every day, arm aloft, the grin.
'Erm someone else… no, not you, Standing.'

'Sir, sir, I've got a rubber stuck up my nose, sir.'

But here's a question for you, Keith – how did it go? Not
the extraction of that tough khaki-green lozenge, but all those
after school activities – your late teens, employment, raising
a family, bank statements, the long haul, your life?

You can put your hand down now.

# Orion

You have to see me to believe me or so I'm told.
I was up there when Dorothy was writing her journal:
*Moonlight lay upon the hills like snow.*
                                        Examine me now
and remember how your father fixed my position
in his calculations over Essen before the incendiary drop.
He thought I'd gone, but I came back for him years later,
unceremonious, no big deal, after that poached egg
on toast he'd fancied and a Sunday repeat of *Morse*.
On his side of the bed I touched him – sent him tumbling
past the face of the alarm clock, luminous, circa half
four in the morning. Had he been able to part the curtains
he'd have spotted me back up there, a nonchalant thief
on a clear night lining up for the identity parade, ready
to hold his gaze as sirens and blue flashing lights broke the peace.

# Tour

After all the rigmarole – certification, house clearance, crem, the final scattering – there's just this tacky plastic concertina of a wallet to show for you. A different heading at the top of each expandable compartment: car, bank, insurance, war pension, licences. We think it's all there, but hidden away in a top drawer under coils of M&S socks and pants, we find an address book, clover green, dimpled, the size of an old petrol lighter.

On the back inside cover a list of targets from the tour you survived: Gelsenkirchen, Essen, Stettin and so on. Also, in your precise angled hand, black ink gone mauve, other stuff: digs, crew, first names of women crossed out, addresses with no postal codes, four digit telephone numbers. Tracer lines of a life before us.

# The Going

*Tattenham Corner 1913*

Last year all the talk was about a filly.
This year there was good money on the King's horse.
We were done up with the best of them.
The sun came on strong. Away from the booths
by the Grandstand over past
the gallops there were larks way up high.

Matt Wake, Phil Connor, Tom Mack –
all of the big names were out there
on the course. The going was officially good
to firm. You don't realise how lush it is,
the grass, how well-watered and green,
how steep the slope is, how much
it falls away at the turn, until you get really close.

Before the starter's call there's a silence
and then the roar. We follow our colours
until they come to our corner
and we were all thrown. A bundle
in black and white through the rails.
Then she went under. Some reared
and then recovered. Near us the glimpse
of a face, wormcasts in hair.

The charge of sound for the last furlong
came over the hill and we ran to catch
a glimpse of the winners being unsaddled
and led up to the rubbing house,
to get the distances, prices, to find out
what all the fuss was about.

# Near Ronda

He came here to breathe –
to live that way must have been
his determination.
Trace a finger through dust
on the marble-topped chest –
from the master bedroom,
crutch-angled, the legs
of two easels, rust-splashed.
Behind stringed piles
of *The Listener*
canvasses face into one
another. A gecko scuttles
across the baked terrace.
Squint into the light
he worked from
a nailed tautness to these
as it took his breath away.
Drawers are wedged
with mauves and lemons,
oxidised solid in their tubes –
a brush you expect to give
flicks against your thumb-nail
brittle as fish-bone.
It used to swim
with the movements
of wind through leaves.

# Locust

Part of some crack marine crustacean airborne fleet,
shorn of antennae, mistaken for a flying lobster
by some shredded Roman gauleiter on the retreat
from North Africa – you are the missing part
of the equation (with no Pythagoras to unpick you),
some low-life extra in an eighties boiler suit
yomping across the stage with your charnel house mates.
Riot shield humour, copper-wire jaws, reinforced
perspex body armour: your crew know just how
to spread the shit: famine, havoc, death… you name it.
From another thousand-plane daylight raid you dump
birds and borers into our gobs; compound eyes in the zone,
riding a dirty hunch, clamped until kingdom come
on your partner's back, short on social skills as a sandstorm,
cranking up again for one last fucking rampage.

# Lines for the Trial of Saddam Hussein

*this dead butcher* – Shakespeare
*he survived for days on Mars Bars in his shallow pit* – CNN


We had some fun over the years. And, yes, I'll happily
talk you through it: underground facilities, the instruments
of restraint, stainless steel gullies for effluence (ash, fat, fibre
and so forth). The palaces would have stood the test of time.
My systems will go on: the irrigation will allow orange-groves,
fruit to pluck. And some day when you flatten out your maps,
trace supply lines, study my blueprints for the people in the marshes,
it'll be me you see, like a watermark on a note held up to the sun. Me,
as you sprinkle chalk-dust to dry black ink from the fat Mont Blanc.

I was right.
        You may nod if you agree.
                I have their names, you know.
The ones who set me up then swung the wrecking-ball, who leaked
the faces of my dead sons. And me, when I emerged from my pit –
incisors inspected as if I were a horse come to market. I allow myself
a smile though at some of you. Twitching like cats in your power naps
as my official face comes out of nowhere into those
air-conditioned quarters.
            The advice is simple: don't flinch –
there are no blows to avoid. Just show due deference, feel the force
of my fingers around your shoulders.
            Brace your spine, stand tall,
plant you feet in the sand.
        Study me.
                Like so.

# Sand Person

*all that remains are stains in the sand*
– Sutton Hoo Information Pack

I challenge you. I live alone
now in symbols: crossed
arrows through a crown.
Then people knew my name.
I had no sword but I led them:
in the face of other forces
I went out to do battle,
staff held high in one hand.

For days after, I swung
on gallows: pelvic girdle
skewed by the pull. Birds
of prey tucked into soft flesh:
they did for me, and some.
Now I'm a shadow curve.
Then people knew my name.
Make me out. I challenge you.

# The Facts of Life

One book given; the other found. The first an HMSO publication. Government-approved guide to puberty – sequences of bodies in black and white, naked, standing, chins raised, ill at ease, palms parallel to hips, faces morphed away to preserve anonymity. Man from boy, woman from girl: genitals, pubic hair as deemed fit for adolescents. Black and white line drawings, regimented, neat diagrams – one option for parents wanting to sidestep awkward questions. A killer of fantasies.

The second initially dwarfed by Churchill's hard-back history of World War Two. Dried glue in spine going – a thin paperback. Emaciated face on the cover. *The Scourge of the Swastika*. A plea and a curse in eyes deep-set beneath shaven head. This must be the author: Lord Russell of Liverpool. And what was a 'scourge'?

The chapter on Dachau gave the answers. When I was getting ready for bed, bits came back: skeletal bodies being bulldozed into pits; pudgy, naked women running past birch trees into a clearing; shrunken, bearded heads from Buchenwald; a boy with a hat on, hands aloft, staring up at the adults in uniform with their guns. Behind them a twister of black smoke.

After this, there was no hiding place. Here were the plain, unbelievable facts. This was what we did.

# Holocaust Exhibition

After, near bolted-
down wooden seats
around the permanent
stall for ice creams,
fries, other junk food,
by the massive guns
and steps up to
the museum, you spot
a dog, shorn, sleek,
giant jaws, off the lead,
strutting its stuff,
heading for
the Lambeth Road,
no sign of a muzzle,
a terrier, male, neck too
thick for a Border,
(a Staffy perhaps?)
power obvious
in his every move.
He angles a pee
against the trunk
of a London Plane,
its leaf-canopy
shadow-dancing
over rain-mottled paths.

No fuss.
        Stain.
                Steam.

Comes
      at his
            master's bidding.

# Namings

*lines after Neruda*

Mondays turn to Tuesdays then weeks to years.
Don't even consider snipping into the hours
With nail-scissors – the names of the days
Will overwhelm you with darkness.

Nobody can really claim to be Will or Dante
Or Beatrice – we are, all of us, specks, molecules,
Drizzled spots of rainwater. Some talk of continents
Or nation-states – what are they frigging on about.
The earth's crust is the only truth and that defies
Any simple tag. Stones clang like bells when I address them.
Roots are a far surer bet than flowers.

Spring drags. It's taken the best part of winter
To get its arse in gear. One year's the history
Of Europe. Time runs barefoot on the cinder-track
At the White City. Set, on your marks – we are
Perpetually new-born. Why fill our mouths that howl
From the off with stumbling blocks of sound,
Modes of address, the rigmarole of titles, and, god
Love us, signatures, possessives?

Asleep, I have no name. Awake,
I'm the same as the man who slept.

## Caspar David Friedrich

No need for an incubus
or massive doses of opium
and raw pork. No murals of Saturn
tearing off toffee-apple heads.

It's simple fare – dawns
and twilights, hands held together
in prayer, solitary prowlers
looking for something coded

in scrub against days' old snow.
Or there in those thin green shoots
you didn't notice at first
by the stones to the crossing.

# Santa

Not some red-gowned fraud in Hamleys, all fake
white beard and seedy laugh. No, a thin saint,
Spanish, stress on the first 'a' – Galicia his place
of birth – there, with his small ring-shaped cake,

in the market square, by a stone fountain,
not wishing to give offence, hair silver-grey,
close-cropped, he nibbles and picks, incognito
in the gabble of stalls, miles away, replaying

an ascent of steps cut back into a cliff-face,
the swell and suck of tide, a trawler's rainbow
spillage, gulls tatty in its wake. On the actual day

he'll eat fish, lift white flesh from feather-trace
of bone, wet slate of skin. Then he'll break
the bread, listen for ages, wait for his god in silence.

## To a Pipistrelle

Forgive us our early evening summer drinks,
our interference to your fine-tuned reception,
our wittering across unoaked Chardonnay,
Stan Getz or Arvo Pärt drifting your way
with the nicknames you won't get (Big Dee,
Hodge-Podge) past sonics and a titter
of accompanying laughter that maybe
draws you down come dusk: full tilt Billy
Whizz, gut-curving bullet dive, liquorice sheen,
an even giggle and then back on up to an Arts
and Crafts chimney, registering an exit to light.

\*

Poetry after all for the amusement of bankers and other sedentary arm-chair people in after-dinner moods. No other.

> T.E. Hulme

Orsino: There's for thy pains (*gives money*).

> Shakespeare

# Prophet

wants to address the queues
for the ranks of black cabs

those striding past the flower-stall
and the Late Prices Standards

outside Charing Cross,
and the harried folk driven, oh

so driven, short-stepping it down
towards the ticket-barriers

for escalators and already-jammed
platforms for District or Bakerloo,

wants to freeze-frame them somehow
and say firmly, not losing his rag,

not in rags or wearing a giant
grinning Blair or Bush mask,

not three-parts-stoned,
not naked, not all sanctimonious

philanthropist, not part of a mass
protest to shut down Canary Wharf,

but in level tones, appreciating
the pressures, with respect

to you and yours, wants to say,
quite simply, you're wrong,

there's nothing at the end of this,
*you're not actually creating anything*

(and no, please don't roll out
the 'wealth creation' comeback ) –

just consider – one day you might stop,
study the paving, the sparrows

pecking round your feet,
and think where it's all taken you

# Regeneration

Samuel Pepys, dubbed the new Cicero, exits
William Hill under the arches at London Bridge
as the call comes: *Get your bets on sharpish – they're going
into the traps.* He's angsting about the Dutch
off Tilbury, those fire-ships, his gold. He's got
by heart *1001 Movies You Must See Before You Die*,
hot-foots it past Poundstretcher and Primark,
a frank exchange with his wife (wisely mute in closet)
fresh in his mind, following last night's expedition
to bury gold. A botched job: rotted bags, coins
gone AWOL, the lot. He was bang on though
about incendiary dumps from Dorniers over
the totem river-snake, cue credits, and can be
moved to ecstasy by Royal Operatics.

What does he do exactly? Something big in the city,
chief recorder of the fire to end all fires, adviser
to head-hunters from his pitch under a patio heater
outside a conference suite ('Central London Location').
On a bit of a roll actually. Chosen theme for next address:
'regeneration'. *All right then babes, press double click.*
Strangers draw fingers down their cheeks: *estoy
a dos velas, estoy a dos velas.* He knows which way
the wind blows, veteran of a pandemic that brought
out the dead in us, driving him up the old A40
to 'The Chequers' at Chalfont Saint Peter
where some veteran pub-quiz bore is closing in
on the punchline of the one about the master
of wit and repartee, and what he says to the clown.

# Borders

Ground Floor between *Fiction* and *Poetry*.
The second time in as many days. It comes at me.
The smell from where she sits between *Travel*
and *Crime* is enough make browsers wrinkle
features in '*what is <u>that</u>?*' disgust. She stinks.

Because clothes for sleeping rough, layer upon
layer, are being walked in, underneath the visible
leather-sheen great-coat and cap. Auschwitz?
That liberation shot at the wire? No, here, beneath
the *3 For 2* CD offers in the Borders Summer Sale.

The truth is she impregnates every last page of verse:
the entire Carcanet list, the brand new Armitage,
the Collected Muldoon, the Selected O'Hara, the new
Billy Childish, *101 Poems That Will Change Your Life* –
you name it. We all track on by, join a queue

to pay by plastic. She exits into Market Square, freeing
up from under the cap her long streak-grey hair,
making her way beyond us. I keep finding her
days later, unremitting, unbearable still, in page
after page of Paul Celan or Miklós Radnóti.

# Settlers

*Cichorium intybus*


    It's on to this patch of municipal earth round
ill-tended birch saplings, that you make it, arrive,
in an instant, seemingly, settle.
                          After broken nights
of rocking and cooing, envious neighbours look down
as they change nappies, get kids into uniform.
On this waste area bounded by a box junction,
'World of Pots' and the London Road, there'd been
a bakery, backyards, 'The Star and Garter', paving-stones
sloshed clear of dregs, ripe garbage in leaky black bin-liners,
queues for a farmhouse, split tins. Now your silence
is a kind of marker – forced to flee river-banks, grassy
inclines, your name morphed in mouths over dust
trails from the east. Passers-by remark just how
smart you are, how street-wise – those pale blue eyes,
for example: energy-saving flowerheads, shut eye
on automatic, come midday heat. Wow. You are sons
of your fathers, retro long-hairs from the seventies –
sporting hairy stiff-looned shanks, burdock-wedges.
You invite study, scuffed kicks, hurled stones sometimes.
Your forebears, the great travellers, have unmarked graves
all down Quarry Hill – they too worked in light
reckoned fabulous, went as far as West Africa,
*'brought back with them gold-dust and other curiosities'*.

You lot might just make it through to September –
a gang-mower and shaven heads the standard fate.

# Personal Empowerment Practice

I engage regularly in prayer and meditation.
I achieve tremendous spiritual satisfaction.
I definitely agree with the above statement.

I have a network of friends and acquaintances.
I am seldom impotent, require only modest medication.
I engage regularly in prayer and meditation.

I absorb new information, can communicate
a sense of dread and other classified data.
I definitely agree with the above statement.

When I want to weep, drink alone, urinate
in public, I climb stairs, take positive action.
I engage regularly in prayer and meditation.

I rarely yearn for colonic irrigation,
comfort-binge, contemplate self-molestation.
I definitely agree with the above statement.

I am seldom impotent, require only modest medication.
I have a network of friends and acquaintances.
I engage regularly in prayer and meditation.
I definitely agree with the above statement.

## *from* 'The Paddington Cantos'

                                                        And…

**xx**

I have told you of how things were under Mrs Bird
                                          in the kitchen
and the true base of credit in Paddington's money-box
                    the abundance of marmalade
on his paws and in jars
and of the goings-on at number thirty-two
                                Windsor Gardens

And Mister Gruber said ' It is easy to shoot past the mark'

bun's prow dipping into cocoa
over elevenses down
                                the Portobello Road
as the young bear extends his grubby paw


**xxi**

And Mister Curry demanded 'Bear! Come over here, Bear,
            lend me a hand with this serving-hatch
            and there'll be
                            sixpence in it for you
I'm going to do a little bit of shopping'

with usura the line grows thick
with usura
is the duffle-coat made sticky with marmalade stains

## xxii

(I should cocoa)

## xxiii

Curry preyed on the young bear
        yelled MAKE IT NEW
Paddington dipped a paw
                into an open jar of marmalade

## xxiv

And then went down to the kitchen
and bashed a hole in the wrong wall
                so that:

# In Brief

*Far away and blue were the Surrey Hills, and the towers
of the Crystal Palace glittered like two silver rods* – H.G. Wells


it's the early summer
   scraggings of buddleia

      glimpsed tops
of horse chestnuts

walled parks spotted
   through dust motes
on commuter trains

empty distant
   gas-holders
   meticulous
Edwardian brickwork

low walls
   caked in soot
bird-cacked in graffiti

the Hawksmoor
   up towards
Limehouse

   those transmission
towers above
   Crystal Palace

that do for me
   over
and over again

# The Opening of the Sixth Seal

The end of the world
and the slave
rejoices.
        Coins litter
broken steps.

*

Even while we watch the boatman mending his sail,
the petroleum is hurting the sea

– David Jones

# Cambridge

*radiant with bovine life* – E.M. Forster


Docks, nettles, self-sown
   sycamores, willows
thunderstruck by their own
   brilliance, sap-boiled,
boughs gone scissor-handed.

*The cow is there, now.*
Do not move suddenly
   or she'll scare.

Scrutinise the lining
   of flies. First thistles
then she tongues down a slip
   of overhanging willow.

She is there.

~

   A woman sleeps rough
by the chained punts, money-spiders
   criss-crossing her back.

~

Attempting steps down
   from Fellows' Court,
the poet, grand old man,
   white-haired with stick.

~

       The living image of my mother
whispers to her companion:
          'I like walking full stop.'

High summer's over.

       The great elms motionless,

yellow blotches on their leaves.

       *I'm there – in the meadow –*
*I have proved it to myself.*

# Socialist Realism

I'd made it – broken the back
of *Anna Karenina* on a three day week
of eight-hour shifts, barely conscious
of the world out there: the lines at Grunwick,
another march by the National Front, the progress
of the exiled Shah. All done in top-floor digs
on the Lensfield Road with a view over a carpark
and a criminal Edwardian fire escape.

Only the one official walk out – to The Oak,
an Irish dive by the lights, creamy pints
of stout skimmed by a blunt plastic cut-throat.
Fats Domino declared his own free state
on Blueberry Hill. Oliver's army was here
to stay. Talk with Alan and Moore over
the chicken chow mein was of 'narodnost'
and our commitment to the cause. Then
to the place of labour: working flat out
on bed or floor, a production line of hand-rolled
borstal specials and Maxwell House brews
from the communal tin.
                                       Snow drifted through
the second night; an easterly wind jittering
the string of the primitive extractor fan.
History had become one vast steppe. By dawn,
water at Hobson's Choice was laminated in ice.

My classic set in Linotype Pilgrim fell apart
at the death– individual leaves came away
in my hands from the creased black spine.
The only thing to stick was an image of Kitty
and Levin under the Milky Way before the run
of blank sheets you get at the very end.

## Reading Yeats in The Granta

What rough beast...
                Jon Tipple, isn't it,
all randy laughter, *Eraserhead* hair,
     fingering shrapnel from the till,
           proffering another pint of *Abbot*.

Love's bitter mystery...
              the faintest trace
of down on an arm can do it. T-bone, fillet or rump.
     'Green leaf or mixed? Any dressing for the salad?'
        Grant me an old man's frenzy.

What else have I to spur me into song?
                  Ah, there, across
the mill-pond towards the new Pizzeria,
     those punters with that bloody great pole
          playing silly buggers next to a swan.

# The Cambridge Ghost

I'm not down some
grey-muzzled road
off the old Kite

nor chalked up
with REFRESHMENTS
and ICES beneath

a pyramid
of canned peas
there since rationing

nor standing any week-day
dusk by a temporary
bus stop on Pound Hill

nor head-down
over the drop handlebars
of some five-gear

Gentleman's Racer
sporting tweeds
and cycle-clips

nor behind a crack-pot
hollyhock by spiked black
railings past the U.L.

but simply blistering off
in globules
that have collected

according to the laws
of surface tension
on the bonnet

of a permit-holder's Polo
under paving-stone-
cracking sycamores

down Grange Road
contemplating that turn
up to The Maltings

# False Oat Grass – A Figure of Eight Walk
*for Amanda*

Crawling boards circa nineteen forty five,
Dutch ladders, lethality and vulnerability
Testing equipment for Blenheims, concrete
Posts, lichen-scored, collapsed timberwork
Among teasels, miked up, like sea holly,
Choco-rust, re-inforced poppy bunker blocks,
Coins, nerve-centres for ballistics, timing
Beacons, copper thieves, control freak desks –
*Basically they bombed the shit out of it*,
Shingle and military kit, and lo on a level
The long glory of tankers watch-strapped
To the sea-line, jellyfish pagoda, abrupt
Shingle plunge, swales, contorted riveting,
Native speakers, *all on the website, I expect*:

All on the website, riveting native speakers,
Contorted swales, abrupt shingle plunge,
Jellyfish pagoda, I expect, watch-strapped
To the sea-line, the long glory of tankers
And lo on a level, shingle and military kit,
(*Basically they bombed the shit out of it*);
Control freak desks, copper thieves, timing
Beacons, nerve-centres for ballistics, coins,
Re-inforced poppy bunker blocks, choco-
Rust, collapsed timberwork in teasels, like
Sea holly, miked up, concrete posts lichen-
Scored, lethality and vulnerability testing
Equipment for Blenheims, Dutch ladders,
Crawling boards circa nineteen forty five.

# Easterly

Lanterns outside The Harbour Inn are visible
come noon from the marshes off Buss Creek.
We crawl behind a trailer-load of beet, shapes fresh
out of cold earth. Creatures at the side of the road curl
like the ones in Narnia turned to stone
by the White Witch – you half-expect them to stretch,
get up and saunter away into the dark stitch
of hawthorn and briar. We're heading east,
hoping to miss the Christmas rush. Another game
of Animal, Vegetable or Mineral is called for.
Heaped bags of Coalite glow unreally on a forecourt
by Darsham Holt. Headlights are set on dipped.
Walkers trudging up along the Blyth's raised bank
are elongated against the red-barred sky
like the soldiers in Lean's 'Great Expectations',
the old black and white one, when they fan out
in the hunt for the convicts. It's the weather
for shelter, a bundle of shivers, brandy, that pie.

# Short Stay

The buggy-pusher in a parka
zigzags across the beach.
Breakers are 'awesome' out there.

Three-storey pebbledash
denotes the front:
at Summerleaze

a turned sign
indicates 'Vacancies'.
Fresh rust has been

carefully spray-painted
under each satellite dish.
From behind double-glazing

a woman in a tight grey
bubble-perm sees out
another day from

her floral armchair.
A crushed bottle
of Lucozade promises

'Brain and Body Energy'.
The plaque on this bench
ends 'Till We Meet Again.'

The clocks go forward next week.
I'll give it a few seconds more
before I make tracks.

# Near Death

Mainly in cars – the dazed pedestrian,
the 'actual' emergency stop, the faulty
accelerator cable, the suicide bid
(navigating minus glasses by a Thames mist
all the way back from Shepperton) –

but the closest was aged four
in Aix-en-Provence when only an aura
of innocence found me alive come dawn,
nuzzling and stroking the sleek hair
and floppy ears of the chained guard dog
that monitored our overnight motel,
oblivious to the gnawed femur
and the bowl of stale metallic water.

# The Other Poet's House

A massive Rothko
dominates
the stairwell.

Over a fish curry
talk drifts to what next
in the Middle East.

From the guest room
on the top floor
past 'historic' quays

and the estuary's curves
glistening like an eel
you know the moor's there.

Tomorrow you'll drive
out alone, around dawn,
with some early Van the Man

after a bit of wild stuff –
gale-racked hawthorn,
lichen-pocked stone.

The works.

# Hair of the Dog

warmth still in the air
and huge hanging baskets
of geranium and fuchsia
drip onto the cobbles
outside The Lamb and Flag –

Lazenby Court, WC2,
where Dryden and Rochester
used to go out on the razz,
and here time's nowhere near
being called despite lengthening

shadows of assembled punters
edging the ancient stones
and already I'm mapping out
the day for us to hold this all
in retrospect – the warm air,

the hanging baskets, the water
on the cobbles – when you clap me
on the shoulder with a rolled-up copy
of *The Economist*, big grin under
steel-grey mop, hail me – *Peter*

and time ahead of us is sensed –
the knowledge now that we'll continue
well past a first pint of *Pedigree*

# The Great Elk

Actually this one played
up front for West
Bromwich Albion
and scored with a towering
back-stick header
in injury time away at Leeds.

# Sweetman

Provider of bonbons, wine gums and lemon sherbets
from grease-proof paper bags stowed in the inside pocket
of a quilted anorak, thus christened 'Sweetman' by us,

located in E-Block mid-terrace regardless of
opposition (Grimsby in the Cup, their lads chanting 'Fishermen,
Fishermen, Fishermen', Wolves, Man City, the Baggies…),

which evening game was it that you melted away from,
long-striding it after a nil-one reverse, feeling in
anonymous sugar-dust for another predictable mouthful?

# Bin Men

Sometimes you'll mutter
in your sleep
at their engine rumble
before the closer clatter
and purr of containers
being shaken out and tipped
like Foreman dumped
for the mandatory count
after that right lead from Ali.

Men purposeful
as beaters at a hunt
hitch a lift on the rear
of the compressor.
Cut to natural light.
And it's all gone
like a dream
to landfill sites
under gulls scrapping
flickering like eyelids
in REM, scavenging
over vast bin-linered pits.

## After George Trakl

Come evening you can tune into bat shrieks.

Two black horses frisk and buck around the fields.

There's the rustling of leaves from the red maple tree.

The wanderer makes out lights from a pub up ahead.

Bloody awesome! The taste of wine from a bottle
just cracked open, a handful of salted nuts.

It's wonderful – to lurch and sway pissed as a fart
through this forest invaded by darkness.

Doom-laden bells toll away from out there past
these black branches.
                        Dew accumulates on his face.

# The Goodbye Game

Pick a rendezvous – this crypt off Trafalgar Square will do. Allow others to concentrate on vegetable broth, organic bread. Now add a decade or so of estrangement (not forgetting lunch hour weeping fits in assorted fields around south Buckinghamshire). Apply midday heat to Duncannon Street, pavements bone-dry, no chance of give-away mud or leaf-smears to blow the 'great aunt' alibi.

Next, concentrate on the profile of a face, duly note soft down on cheeks, grey hair near temples, a puffiness around the lips. Try to block out the tap-tapped cigarette, posed 'jazz era' exhalations of smoke. Roll the dice into language. You might turn up 'I missed you,' or 'I never stopped thinking about you,' and how about 'I'm sorry, I'm not wearing clean knickers.'

Endgame: you are the last two players, only you know the rules. Remember the importance of coded references. To test this system try 'switchbacks' or 'Nork Park' or 'the gallops' and to make absolutely certain, reference 'a dog called Bastard'.

You'll both sense when time's up. No need for anything but that last eye contact at the zebra crossing over the Strand, then head-down strides up into Charing Cross, clocking platform information, on through automatic ticket barriers, up to electronic doors. Push the red button: they'll open with a hiss.

## Your Hands

                        might even have come
from a bird of prey,
like the massive buzzard
we once saw from the 303, circling
close to Stonehenge,

                      their ancient calluses
a lizard texture, palms lined
like a turtle's head, digits
nicotine-stained into Italian fig tones.

You were forever gripping –
for eating-irons, keys, the remote
control – like a blind man
without a stick.

                  Towards the very end,
lungs holed by cancer, downstairs
on a camp-bed set up by a torpedo
of oxygen, you still jittered
                              for a last illicit
Silk Cut, to be taken at the backdoor,
one long-nailed hand clutching
at a jamb as you puffed away
                              up into the night.

# Nightwatchman

*an elegy*

Mouth set. So far, nought
not out, having dabbed at
the spinner who'd been giving it
some air. Hands soft – taking the sting
out of each delivery.

Their demon quickie
is brought back into the attack.
                He pounds in.
A virtuoso leave.
                You judge the away
swinger to perfection.

Shadows nudge further east
across the square. Pigeons clatter
as mid-off jogs back. Thunderous
approach to the wicket. This one
you nick.
            The keeper whoops and hurls
the ball to the skies. You walk without waiting
for the dreaded finger.
                      Head-down trudge
to a sealed cube with the door marked
VISITORS. Dust motes patrol heated air.

In among the grim socks, grass-stained
whites and open coffins you take in
the smell of embrocation, shake off
gloves, stoop to unbuckle your pads.

# Beautiful Game

*a found poem*

I was playing football
in the grounds
of this rather grand house

with Kandinsky,
Macke and Paul Klee.
Anyway, August sends over

a cross and I meet it
with my head,
a decent enough

contact and there
and then
the ball bursts

into roses, red ones,
millions of them,
petals everywhere.

*

# Gift

*after a line by Mandelstahm*


A body. My very own possession –
what am I to make of you?
Devoted life-partner, let me know
who to thank. Involuntary father

confessor to my thousand secrets –
the crop circles of eczema,
the crisis of thinning hair –
comforter through night terrors,

you give me the freedom
to hold up a finger, thus,

and say I touch the sky.

## NOTES

'Orion' – The 'Dorothy' in line two is Dorothy Wordsworth.

'The Going' – The centre of the poem, although in the background, is the action of the suffragette Emily Davison on Derby Day, 1913.

'Namings' – This poem is based on Neruda's 'Demasiados nombres'.

'Regeneration' – 'Estoy a dos velas': Spnaish: literally 'down to two candles' ('I'm skint').

'Settlers' – Thanks to Charlie Evans for the following information: Chicory *Cichorium intybus*. Medium/tall perennial, hairy or not; stems stiff, well balanced, no milky juice. Leaves pinnately lobed, the upper undivided. Flowerheads clear blue, 25-40 mm, in leafy spikes; June-Sept. Grassy and waste places.

'The Opening of the Sixth Seal' – Based on a painting by Francis Danby (National Gallery of Ireland).

'Cambridge' – The epigraph and ideas start from the opening of E.M.Forster's 'The Longest Journey' and the discussion about the existence of objects (based on G.E. Moore's philosophical ideas), in this case, cows.

'False Oat Grass' – The setting is the spit at Orford Ness.

'Hair of the Dog' – This poem is dedicated to Nigel McNelly

'After George Trakl' – An improvisation on his 'Zu Abend Mein Herz'.

'Your Hands' – This poem is dedicated to David Knight.

'Nightwatchman' – An elegy for my father.

'Beautiful Game' – This follows a dream recounted by James Cockburn, artist.